LORD MAITREYA CONVEYS

The Reemergence of Atlantis

LORD MAITREYA

& Rohan Sewaney

LORD MAITREYA CONVEYS

The Reemergence of Atlantis

Cover image: Dr Martina Violetta Jung

Cover arrangement: Kirsten Lenz

Edited by Katharina Adari

www.rohansewaney.com

www.namasyouniversity.org

PREFACE

I am MAITREYA. I have been with Earth since 3 million years. I have been working with humanity and critical missions ever since. I work with the SANAT KUMARA, the spiritual head of the Earth and all kingdoms inhabiting Earth. I am happy to announce that this book marks the first of its series. My focus for humanity is to help them execute their soul missions, provide guidance, and assist them in the coming of the New Age. I represent the human kingdom in Shambala.

I helped Yeshua by providing messages for humanity. I guided him in his incarnation to fulfill his mission. I had incarnated on Earth as Krishna, helping humanity expand their consciousness. I was Maitreya in my most recent incarnation, where I spread the messages of love and light.

The coming of the New Age is inevitable. It will happen if you choose to ascend or not. With this book, I want each of you to realize the opportunity that awaits you and how you can shift to New Earth in this incarnation.

I love and bless you all!
MAITREYA

LORD MAITREYA CONVEYS

CONTENTS

The Reemergence of Atlantis

THE TIME OF ATLANTIS

I lived during the time of Atlantis; it was a golden period. I was one of the few who witnessed its downfall. I did not realize the enormity of it until I went through it on Earth. It was a golden period and meant a spiritual peak for humanity. By spiritual peak, I mean humanity knew the deepest spiritual teachings, which are currently lost. These teachings meant everything to people, and they lived by it their entire lives. I also embodied these teachings during Atlantis, but no one saw coming what was about to happen. An envelope of darkness engulfed our planet from all sides. We could not see or run from it; it was that fast. But what exactly happened, you may ask? It resulted from a few individuals' wrongdoings, which sank the entire kingdom. It marked the deepest sad moment for the rest of us while we looked at it engulfing civilization as a whole, leaving no one behind. It was a time of true despair and sadness. We never thought of how we could overcome it. Today we ask you, whatever we lost during that time, to build it back with us. We have the chance to do so now. We have volunteers from across the galaxy helping us right now, you being one of them. Collectively, we can manage to establish Atlantis again. We want to work with you all to establish the essence of the Golden Age. It can only happen if we all collectively act together and build it from scratch. The technologies waiting to come forward must also be invented on Earth. It will happen soon. The scenario of Earth will change like never before, and we are delighted to say that.

We, along with our Off-Earth Allies, would build it. Our friends from across the galaxy are waiting as well to contribute. Our Off-Earth Allies comprise beings from Sirius, Pleiades, Arcturus, Andromeda, and many more. Sirius and Pleiades have been our old friends, helping for many years with consciousness expansion. We love to work with them. They are now on Earth in numerous numbers to help us expand consciousness. Many incarnate aspects work with them. Many are also waiting to work with humans, but due to the law of free will, they cannot interfere unless humans ask.

Atlantis was not just a country or religion or a continent. It was a collective; the entire human population was called Atlantis. There was no separation between individuals; each considered the other as self, i.e., a fragment of God. Each individual believed God to be within and knew the truth of unity consciousness. People had no fear; they knew that nothing could happen to them; it could only happen to their bodies. Everyone had love for each other. Atlantis was one of the great civilizations of our galaxy, but because of certain mistakes, it eventually fell. Atlantis was inhabited by various species who all lived in close relationship with humans. These creatures you only know from mythology. Some consider them real, but the rest still consider them a fragment of human imagination.

The creatures you have known for a few years, like dragons, fairies, elves, centaurs, and so forth, are real and coexist with us, but humanity cannot see them because of a blocked third eye, which is essential to see them. For instance, dragons help us maintain the life-force energy of Earth. You may not completely understand their purpose, but they exist in realms where humans cannot enter. These realms are called nature stations of Earth. They visit us through these stations and return back to their realms. There are hundreds of nature stations on Earth, and humans are unaware of them. They may have passed by a nature station unknowingly, getting a strange feeling while crossing it, but they have not taken the time to study it more, know its purpose, and find out how to contact these beings when near a nature station.

A nature station is a gateway to nature beings; it is a portal. Beings from either side can visit their side of the portal. However, it is usually nature beings visiting us through these portals mainly because humanity is still unaware of them at a larger scale. Humanity needs knowledge on how to communicate with these beings, mainly dragons, fairies, elves, phoenixes, centaurs, and others. These beings were incorporated into human imagination so that humanity at least knew of them even if they had not seen one. The stories you read about them were divinely orchestrated on levels the human mind cannot comprehend but can at least understand their concept. Humanity still has a long way to go in order to accept these beings as inhabitants of planet Earth. Many interact with them but keep it a secret because they know people will not believe them unless they interact with one. It is human nature to accept things purely based on logic; we do not blame them since they have been mass-conditioned since childhood to think in a certain way. Although this way helps people deal with the world, it greatly affects pursuing one's own spiritual journey.

Spirituality, being the construct, needs faith and trust more than anything else. Without faith, you are lost trying to make sense of things in your mind while your mind is not designed to calculate future possibilities. The human mind cannot completely comprehend future events. These events result from one's karma, desires, and actions. Unless and until you do not have karma for certain events to be experienced, you cannot experience them. That is the law, no matter how hard you try to manifest. Once you have karma for an event to be lived, you need to choose to live that event, meaning you should have a desire for that event. Until you do not choose, it is not available to you. Next is action; that is correct: action is important as well. Just choosing is not enough; you need to act on your desires. Only then can the event occur. Few events occur because they are destined in one's life, irrespective of the above. One's own soul carefully chooses these events before incarnation to learn certain lessons or activate certain behavioral patterns for one's life. This pattern can have many purposes, like introducing humbleness in one's life so that an incarnated aspect of the soul can take care of future responsibilities. Behavioral pattern changes are needed in one's life to fulfill one's life's purpose successfully. One's soul introduces these patterns before or during incarnation. Let me give an example: A certain person is destined to lead an organization in the future. However, due to current behavioral patterns, the person does not seem fit to lead, even in the future. Therefore, one's soul might introduce an event into the incarnated aspect of that soul's life to trigger a behavioral change. This behavioral change is required long term to lead the organization. You all must have experienced these kinds of events in your life on Earth for you to exhibit the qualities needed most in the future.

The Reemergence Of Atlantis

Atlantis, a civilization of history; some have heard, some have not. When I say reemergence of Atlantis, I do not necessarily mean the actual Atlantis of the past. By reemergence, I mean the coming of the Golden Age back on Earth. Atlantis is an integral part of the history of Earth, but that does not mean the New Age will be exactly like Atlantis. Humanity may recreate in similar ways or create something authentic with a foundation similar to Atlantis. By foundation, I mean similar values, knowledge, understanding of cosmic laws, and relationship with the Source. It is difficult to explain in words, but I will try to explain the concept as closely as I can in the coming chapters, where I briefly speak about the Source, the relationship of oneself with the Source, and what you can do during this time to bring back the Golden Age. Golden Age means an age of advanced and matured souls who have graduated to the next level of consciousness. It can be achieved now during this time on Earth.

Earth has not been in a place like this before. We had to take numerous actions for Earth to enter the Golden Age. The first step was to ensure that the planet inhabited high vibrations, i.e., that Earth's people were in a high-vibration state. This state was achieved via numerous initiatives across the globe. One of the major initiatives was Brahma Kumaris, a spiritual organization in India, which the SANAT KUMARA himself led as the walk-in of selected people. The walk-in representatives have a huge following today. They have reached millions in India and beyond from numerous centers worldwide. Brahma Kumaris' prime goal was to create an environment for people to reach high vibrations for Earth to have a chance to enter the Golden Age directly, and it was able to serve its purpose in numerous ways. In 1987, Earth passed its test to enter the Golden Age directly, and we got a ticket to transform Earth and its inhabitants.

The process was not simple; it meant hardships for representatives of Brahma Kumaris. It meant a great deal of discipline and commitment. This type of commitment had never been shown on such a large scale on Earth. Few have come close, but none like Brahma Kumaris. The organization means a lot to Shambala and the SANAT KUMARA, with the SANAT KUMARA being the prime architect and creator of Brahma Kumaris. Since then, it has evolved in many stages and will do so in the coming few decades with the help of Shambala and chosen incarnate aspects of souls who have taken an important mission of leading the organization, with Rohan Sewaney being one of them. Shambala and the SANAT KUMARA himself have chosen him. His role is to act as a vessel for me to provide teachings waiting to come from us and the SANAT KUMARA. The role is not a small one. He has to act as a guide for the teachings of the New Age to come forth. The time to awaken is now; it does not matter how much progress you have made. As part of these teachings, you will reach the next level of consciousness. These teachings were not allowed to be provided earlier. Now, this knowledge will be provided to each soul on Earth, given that they are open to receiving it. The coming of the Golden Age is here, my friends; it's time to act now. The teachings will reach the people they are supposed to reach. They will reach millions around the world. With that being said, take these teachings seriously and try to live by these teachings every single day of your life. Concluding, together, we will build the New Earth with new teachings provided by the SANAT KUMARA and myself to the people of Earth. The SANAT KUMARA is speaking through Dr Martina Violetta Jung, a German national whom he has walked into. She also provides new teachings coming forward and has a major role in awakening humanity. Together, Martina and Rohan form the leadership team of NAMAS YOUNIVERSITY, with Martina being the co-teacher and walk-in for the SANAT KUMARA and Rohan being the co-teacher and walk-in for me – Lord MAITREYA.

The teachings coming forth from these two will act as divine knowledge waiting to come forth for New Age transformation. Brahma Kumaris, the organization with the prime mission of leading everyone back to the Golden Age, has a major role to play for India and beyond. A few will resist the new teachings since they challenge current beliefs—the beliefs of the old Earth, separation from God, and being different from God. But when I say New Earth cannot come without these teachings, it is vitally important to understand that old teachings were true for the time they were given, but now we can share new teachings since a new time has come. If you feel suspicious or have doubts, it is completely fine since the old teachings are still familiar to you. But you have to let go. By letting go, I do not mean letting go of all the teachings; by letting go, I mean building this knowledge on top of it and trying to understand from a neutral standpoint the motive and the message behind new teachings. Allow me to initiate these teachings. Have an open mind and try to absorb them. Read my words again if you do not seem to grasp the knowledge, but never leave it midway since these teachings will form the basis of the Golden Age.

THE SANAT KUMARA

The SANAT KUMARA has been the spiritual head of Earth for almost 19 million years. He has helped sustain Earth and the evolving beings inhabiting Earth, leading them closer to the Source. The SANAT KUMARA is a position of Earth taking responsibility for all souls on Earth in different dimensions. Taking such a huge responsibility for so many souls is not easy. The SANAT KUMARA came to Earth 19 million years ago as a humble servant of God. He graciously accepted the mission of being of service to the souls on Earth and Earth itself. He carefully observed the patterns of beings inhabiting Earth. It was a difficult task, but he accepted and laid out big plans for the future of Earth.

Now, during the time of the shift, few challenges lay ahead for Earth. These are humongous tasks that need a lot of support from outside. Yes, I am talking about you. You all agreed to come at the request of the SANAT KUMARA. He made a humble request in front of the Galactic Federation of Light. The Galactic Federation of Light agreed to help with many volunteers from different star systems like the Pleiades, Sirius, Andromeda, Arcturus, Orion, and many more. The maximum number of volunteers came from Orion. I am from the Orion constellation as well and have led many lives there.

I came here three million years ago when Earth needed help to sustain itself. I came with many friends like Yeshua (aka Jesus). We had accomplished great projects during the time of Atlantis. Yeshua and I have had many incarnations together, the most recent being that of Jesus of Nazareth and Lord Maitreya.

The SANAT KUMARA has taken responsibility for the evolution of all souls on Earth, and this shift is one of the major milestones to be accomplished. We at Shambala and the SANAT KUMARA work day and night to make this happen. You may think that this shift in frequency, being a divine task, will happen naturally, but it is meant to be achieved by you all, all people of Earth, and Shambala collectively. We all are meant to bring it back. The SANAT KUMARA, a deva soul from Venus, has a lot of experience and divine qualities that help us assist humanity in its evolutionary plan. The divine plan is something that comes from the Source. We decide the details of its execution. We sincerely commit to this plan and work with enlightened souls for planning and execution. We at Shambala take care of everything.

Shambala is the place from where I am speaking to you right now. It is a city on Earth that humans cannot see. Only if they are provided help by us they enter. It is an evolutionary center. From here, we carefully manage the evolution of souls and devise plans to keep humanity and other kingdoms on the right path. We make many plans here at Shambala, Brahma Kumaris being one of them. We at Shambala planned to establish Brahma Kumaris. We made big plans for Earth's ascension, but most were in vain. Only a few of them succeeded. And through these few successful initiatives, I am able to speak to all of you now. We found a group of dedicated and mature souls to represent us in the dense physical of Earth. Rohan Sewaney represents me, Lord MAITREYA, in the dense physical, and Dr Martina Violetta Jung represents the SANAT KUMARA. Together they form the leadership team of NAMAS YOUNIVERSITY. The goal of NAMAS YOUNIVERSITY is to reach 25 percent of the human population in next three to four decades for the New Age to come soon. We immensely trust Rohan and Martina and would like you all to do the same. They are volunteers appointed by us at Shambala, where all divine missions of Earth are carefully planned, designed, and executed by highly advanced and mature beings of light. Please have faith and trust us when we say that the coming of the New Age depends on the successful execution of missions devised by Shambala. Together with us, Rohan and Martina will form the leadership of New Earth, and all the teachings that are supposed to be established will come from them or their teams. With this divine mission, we hope that you all place your trust in them and us.

We at Shambala carefully observe and oversee all the events happening on Earth. We have been assisting Earth for eons now and will do so in the future. These events are carefully supervised and deeply analyzed for their impact. We know the effects of all Earth events and what they mean for each soul. When you experience or observe earthquakes, tsunamis, or other natural disasters that cause much damage to humanity, it is rebalancing, a rebalancing Earth desperately needs. You may wonder what would be the reason for such events; it is simple – Earth is meant to be home to all living beings inhabiting the planet. If any one group tries to control resources for their selfish use, resulting in scarcity or a difficult environment for other living beings, then Earth takes a decision to rebalance. It has been doing so for thousands of years now, but humanity has not learned its lessons from this and is still trying to control other species and resources for selfish purposes. It saddens us to see this happening on a global scale.

In essence, the SANAT KUMARA has been working with the divine souls who came here to enlighten people. The SANAT KUMARA, along with us, orchestrated the plans made to uplift humanity. The SANAT KUMARA was a guiding force for these divine souls. I would like to emphasize that the missions of incarnated aspects of souls were not easy at all. All the missions require great commitment and dedication. These missions were meant to be accomplished by souls willing to go the extra mile for humanity—and sometimes give more than asked. All these souls had this in common. These missions were not meant to be executed by faint-hearted souls but by experienced ones who had done similar work before and were willing to do so again. The plans made for them would only work under such conditions.

You all are meant to go the extra mile while helping humanity with this phase of its evolution. It is about embodying the Creator, the Source within you, and letting it work through you. The qualities within you are waiting for you to access them. The Divine lies within you. It is not a coincidence that you are reading this book right now. It is meant to reach you. We at Shambala have divinely orchestrated this and would love your support for our mission to awaken humanity. It is not going to be easy, but fulfilling for your soul. The Divine waits for you. The coming of the New Age is imminent; it will come, but we have to bring it; we have to do it – together!

The help that has reached Earth from outside has already been provided in huge numbers. The volunteers are incarnated with an aspect of their soul on Earth. These volunteers are our hope, nothing else. The volunteers need to step up because if they do not, the New Age will not be possible for Earth. We will have to resort to ways that may harm many souls' evolutionary journey, and they may get stuck in this density or dimension for more eons. The reason why the volunteers' work is so important is because they need to awaken other souls. If our volunteers failed, the souls that do not awaken will have to start anew on another planet, in another realm similar to Earth and with similar conditions of suffering and divine imbalance. It would be unwise not to help these souls awaken to the coming of the Golden Age. It remains imminent that souls who want to awaken will do so now. Souls who want to stay asleep will be stuck in similar conditions of suffering and despair until they decide to move along on their evolutionary path. We want to help all souls to awaken to their true selves. It is crucial – now.

LORD MAITREYA

Most of you might be aware of my duties in this ascension process. If you are not, let me explain my role and responsibilities. I am commonly known as Lord MAITREYA by human incarnate aspects of souls. My true name, my soul's name, is different from the one you know.

I have had many incarnations on Earth since the time of Atlantis. I have had roles of a priest, a warrior, a teacher, and many more, which do not need to be disclosed. My responsibility as LORD MAITREYA is to help human souls evolve towards the Source and assist them where needed. I take this responsibility very seriously. I am one of the few on Earth who have helped humanity grow closer toward God and enlightenment as a World Teacher. I did so by working together with incarnate aspects of souls who established various teachings. However, the teachings have been manipulated by humanity when passed on to the next generations over thousands of years. The teachings initially given by me were different from what you read today. They are not exactly what I and we in Shambala wanted to convey. I have been working since to bring back the initial teachings offered to humanity as well as new teachings that are desperately needed during this time of ascension. New teachings were not allowed to be disclosed earlier due to Earth being in a lower-density state as well as cosmic laws restricting us from disclosing it to humanity.

I want to acknowledge the help of incarnate aspects of souls because these teachings are being conveyed to you directly by me through them. I wish more volunteers would join us so that the ascension of human souls would be successful and smooth. I wish to convey that I am one of the voices on Earth along with the SANAT KUMARA, who primarily speaks through Dr Martina

Violetta Jung. The SANAT KUMARA's role is to help humanity by sharing up-to-date information about this shift, and teachings that can help humanity evolve faster. I and the SANAT KUMARA will work with Rohan and Martina to provide these teachings. I am very happy and excited to work with them to pass these true and up-to-date teachings on to humanity.

I will start with my teachings on the YouTube channel NAMAS YOUNIVERSITY, where I currently speak through Katharina Adari along with Master Teachers YESHUA, MOTHER MARY, and SAINT GERMAIN. My primary goal is to spread these teachings worldwide so that they reach the souls they are meant to find in order for them to start taking the necessary steps for their ascension.

I have specific topics to be disclosed to humanity. I want to start with information on the Source as well as us, our relationship with the Source, and the evolutionary process of souls to reach the Source. The process is complicated but can be simplified using examples I shall provide. But it is not about these examples. They should be understood as a means to enhance the understanding of the divine process. I will also cover topics related to the Deva of Humanity, aspects of Atlantis that can be conveyed for better spiritual understanding, as well as practical information for the self-realization process. What I talk about in this book remains valid for this century. All teachings need to be updated. Older teachings were good for their time and immensely helpful to people during that time. Now is the time for ancient teachings to be updated so that the evolution of human souls can happen smoothly.

THE SPIRITUAL REVOLUTION

The Spiritual Revolution on Earth has been in the works for many centuries now. When we were given a chance to build Earth once again like it was during the time of Atlantis, we were quite delighted. The idea of bringing back the Golden Age of Earth was exciting for many but simultaneously meant a humongous task for us to accomplish. We formed teams and started thinking about different ways to accomplish it. No one on the team had worked on such a humongous task before. But we never doubted ourselves and started taking steps towards the plan. For us, it meant working day and night to find incarnated aspects of souls who can work with us from dense physical so that we can work through them.

Earth is a difficult planet where even volunteers who agreed to come to Earth with a plan have completely forgotten their mission. We struggled a lot, but eventually, a handful of people with much support from our side agreed to work with us. This handful of people first needed to be trained to speak with us and trust us with the decisions we wanted them to make. After a few years of training, they started working with us on critical projects. We have been working with them for a few years now. They have our full trust and support.

A huge number of volunteers who had big missions to fulfill left during their training period or when they realized their mission and were too afraid to take it up. Earth has been difficult for them, and we do not blame them. The parameters of Earth make it difficult to go against mass conditioning in all walks of live. I am sure you have faced challenges of that kind.

However, there are some volunteers brave enough to take a stand and they are the ones through whom we are working now in the dense physical. These people agreed to leave their old life behind and establish the foundation of a New Age. These are the volunteers through whom we are speaking right now.

With this book, I want each one of you to realize your own upcoming mission. Each of you, whom this book reaches eventually, has a mission. Due to the veil of forgetfulness, you have forgotten about it. But I and we in Shambala remember all your missions to help Earth flourish again and the few of you who will directly work with us. I want to give you some history and a little background that will help you expand the library of your mind and let you build a foundation for your new journey.

Our Beautiful History

There was a time on Earth when souls lived in unity. There were no separate countries and groups of people that you have now. This was the time of Atlantis. A lot of us had incarnated during this period. If you want to compare the time of Atlantis with the current period to make it understandable, it was a Golden Age on Earth. Atlantis was a place where unity remained in people. I had incarnated as well during the period of Atlantis. Most of you had incarnated as well. It was a place where people cared for each other, understood the relationship with other kingdoms, nurtured people, and understood their connection with the Source that dwells in each of us. Humanity had evolved a lot but reached a plateau. People tried finding new answers in technology rather than in spirituality. Technology evolved to a great extent, and we witnessed the fall of Atlantis; it was a terrible day for all of us. We tried to prevent it and gave many chances but with no success. At one point, the fall was inevitable and we accepted the fate. Now you can understand the magnitude of our current task – souls who had incarnated during Atlantis can again live those days of unity and non-duality.

With this book, I will help you realize and awaken your true self to enter the Golden Age. If you follow this book's teachings wholeheartedly, it will be much easier for you to enter the Golden Age. The teachings of this book have been carefully compiled and personalized for you all. Having trust in my teachings would be the first step. I have divided these teachings into seven parts. Each lesson has equal importance. These teachings are carefully compiled with various Master Teachers, including myself, and agreed upon by everyone at Shambala.

Shambala is the place from where I am speaking right now. It is an evolutionary control center of Earth where we carefully manage the ascension of souls and undertake critical projects to align Earth with the divine plan. I will be covering the divine plan in this book, but for now, you can understand that the divine plan is nothing but the plan created by the Source for the evolution of human souls and other kingdoms that live on Earth along with the soul of Gaia – Zoncriet. During this period of the shift, we can share the divine plan with all of you.

LESSON 1: RELATIONSHIP WITH SOUL

For thousands of years, the concept of the soul has been deformed. The soul is not what many think. The soul is the Source and a fragment of it at the same time. Soul is a unit of the Source that separates from the Source to experience living under different parameters. The Source represents all ideal qualities. These qualities make it the Source. And that is why when we say we are on a journey of return to the Source, in simpler terms, you can say we are on a journey to embody the qualities of the Source. Once you embody those qualities, you will merge back with the Source. I wish it were that simple, but the journey back to the Source requires many lessons, which, when completed, will help the soul reach closer to the Source. On Earth, these lessons can be anything from as small as relationships with friends or as complex as leading a country. The soul itself entirely chooses these lessons. To embody the qualities of the Source, the soul first needs to undergo certain challenges, and only then can the soul embody those qualities. Earth life has a lot of parameters, including but not limited to taking one or many challenges, depending on the maturity of the soul. You have also gone through these challenges in your life, making you question your existence and blame this human life. This is completely natural because unless you do not go through these challenges, you will not get a chance to embody the ideal qualities of the Source, which will help you evolve and move one step closer to the Source.

To help you, the Source has a plan. Earth has a similar plan created by the Source. Adhering to the plan helps us reach the Source; without the plan, we are lost. The divine plan for Earth is to become the 'University Planet of the Galaxy.' Earth will serve as a learning environment for our friends from across the galaxy. Now you know the plan, and with that, my work is done. I am joking. I know it is not as simple as it sounds, but I am happy now that at least you know the ultimate goal we have been trying to achieve. 'University Planet of the Galaxy' signifies a learning school for souls across our galaxy and beyond. Earth will host classes for souls to evolve, learn, and grow. There will be classes like you have in schools and colleges where souls from different parts of the galaxy will attend to learn various subjects. The learning for the soul is never ending until it reaches and reunites with the Source. My colleagues and I are also on this learning journey of returning to Source. And learning is constant no matter how far you are on your spiritual journey. I will present you with an example.

Consider a scholar who has learned everything he could find, which led him to believe that he knows everything. He learned what was made available to him but not everything there is. Earth has a similar story. Until now, we were not allowed to disclose these teachings to you since Earth was under quarantine. But now the quarantine is being lifted daily. The old teachings that were true before no longer hold the entire truth that exists in the Universe and is common knowledge to your souls. This knowledge is so common that it is like walking on a human level. So now you can understand that the knowledge I am trying to impart via this book is already known to your souls, but now is the time to make it known to the incarnated aspects living on Earth as well.

Earth had this knowledge during the time of Atlantis but the knowledge was destroyed gradually, and eventually, humanity was left with nothing. Attempts made by a few enlightened souls effectively maintained trust in the 'Source' you commonly call God or Creator. I want to go more in depth since the concept of the soul's relationship with God has been misinterpreted by many. There are so many versions on Earth that it becomes impossible for an individual to learn the truth of this relationship. Some have learned the truth and were determined enough to find God, but most people rely on their group's teachings. We understand and do not blame them. It is almost impossible to reach the truth of the relationship of one with God. The numerous texts on Earth have some form of truth, but they confuse you more than that they present a consistent theory. There is a reason behind this. The confusion is added deliberately to make you think more and go deeper into the crux of the truth of self-realization and the relationship of yourself with God. Only the ones who were determined enough to clear this confusion found the truth of God within themselves. And there are many examples of that, but I will not list them.

So, what exactly is the relationship of oneself with God? The relationship is exactly like a parent with their children. A child has some qualities of a parent and some of his own. Similarly, the soul has some qualities of the 'Source' and some of its own. But that does not mean the soul is different from the Source. As a parent passes on its DNA to their child, the Source similarly passes on its qualities to the soul. Since a child is similar to his or her parents, a soul is similar to the Source. There is little difference between a child and a soul separated from a parent or Source and trying to find its way back.

The structure of a soul can be better understood as follows: Imagine a fruit. At its core is the seed. Surrounding the core of the fruit is its nourishing flesh. A soul similarly has Source qualities at its core, gathered by experiences it has undertaken. The experiences nourish the qualities of the Source, which are at the core of the fruit. Hence, these experiences are important to the journey back to the Source. I hope with this example, you realize the importance of these experiences, irrespective of their nature. To understand the importance of experiences, I will present you with one more example: Consider your exams. Unless you do not study for exams, you do not attain the knowledge and expertise to be proficient. Similarly, these experiences anchor the development of qualities of Source. Sometimes, the experiences might be tough, but at the end of the day, if you overcome these experiences you are closer to the Source. That explains the tough challenges you might have in this incarnation. Those challenges were meant to test you and anchor the qualities of the Source in you. If you demonstrated the qualities of the Source during those tough challenges, then the experiences would have served their purpose and brought you one step closer to the Source. I hope by now you will have clarity on why these experiences are so crucial for the soul and how they act as an anchor to reach the Source/ Creator/ God.

LESSON 2: RELATIONSHIP BETWEEN GOD AND THE SOUL

Lesson 1 focused on the relationship of oneself with the soul. In Lesson 2, I will focus on the relationship between your soul and God.

Let's start with God. We have many different versions of God on Earth, which vary considerably. Some are similar to one another; some are different from each other. An individual born into a religion believes God to be what religion preaches. But for now, I want to focus on how these teachings came into effect. These teachings were compiled long ago and were updated by generations as and when they felt like adding or removing information. No one was there to stop them or advise them not to change the crux of the teachings. At this age, each religion's teachings have been tampered with. They are not what they were meant to be. The creator of the teachings did not realize that humans would try to tamper with their teachings. This was allowed because of the law of free will on Earth. We are not allowed to infringe upon the free will of humans for them to evolve in a natural environment without other forces trying to interfere. This non-interference pushed humanity into darkness. What we see in today's world is humanity acting out of darkness. It is important for you all to realize that the teachings of each religion have been tampered with by humanity for thousands of years. The concept of God has been reduced to that of a person, figure, or a name. These constructs cannot describe God sufficiently. God is an infinite construct that the human mind cannot completely understand and comprehend. But I will try to explain the concept closest to what and who God is. For that, you will need to keep an open mind and try to absorb it before forming any opinions.

God made us, you and I, and this entire Universe, our

home. The Universe is so big that humanity does not have the technology to measure its vastness. Humanity does not have the tools to see different planets close to Earth because these planets are in other dimensions. For now, consider the Universe to be God. The Universe is so intelligent that the planets and stars are placed exactly where they are supposed to be in order to sustain life. This perfect arrangement is known as God. The perfection in the Universe, your existence, and the existence of billions of organisms together is God. In much simpler words: You are part of the Universe, much like a fish is part of the ocean. If the Universe is God, so are you. You are one of its fragments living life. Are you separate from the Universe? No. Similarly, you are not separate from God. You are God in itself, and along with you, everything there is. So why limit God to a certain figure, name, or personality? I hope this helps you understand the depths of God in you as well as around you.

God dwells within you and me. God dwells in every soul like the example of a child inheriting the DNA and information from its parents. Metaphorically speaking, you have the DNA of God. God is not a separate personality from you, but God dwells within you, your soul. Self-realization happens when you realize this truth. From time to time, enlightened beings have incarnated on Earth to impart the same, but either their teachings were misunderstood or tampered with. The few who came to this realization left the world behind since they knew the truth and they tried to explain it to humanity in vain. People love to cling to old knowledge because they have been told so by their ancestors. And their ancestors were told the same while people kept tampering or misrepresenting the teachings that were meant to be imparted. I hope this clears the way for your understanding and makes you curious in your quest to find God.

LESSON 3: HUMAN INCARNATION AND THE SOUL

You are a human being because you have a human soul. The body is just a costume, but the soul makes you human. The incarnation process is more complicated than most of you think. The costume you are wearing right now is designed for you by your body deva. Devas design our bodies and structures on Earth which we see all around Earth. Even planets are designed by devas. Returning to our topic, the human incarnation is a planned mission that takes a lot of strategy and planning. The person you are today is no coincidence. Your body, gender, and the traits you have are all part of the costume design. Let me tell you how a planning meeting goes for a soul to incarnate on Earth.

First and foremost, the purpose of incarnation is decided, much like your project meetings where the ultimate goal is decided. Once the purpose of incarnation is decided, the parameters to achieve this incarnation are discussed. There are experts who weigh in to decide parameters. These parameters are then agreed upon by the soul who wants to incarnate. Finally, a costume is designed for the soul's lifetime on Earth.

A soul needs to add some kind of challenge to be mastered to anchor the qualities of the Source. The success or failure of an incarnation is decided by whether or not the soul can embody the Source qualities it had planned for. If life on Earth is considered successful, then it is discussed among experts whether the soul would need further lessons on Earth or if it can move to a more advanced planet or realm to learn advanced lessons and embody more qualities of the Source. A human soul, on average, takes about eighty incarnations on Earth to embody the qualities of the Source and move one step closer to God.

In your current incarnation, you must have gone through a few challenges to embark on the path of spirituality. These challenges anchor you to awaken to your true self. You might not believe this, but a few challenges you chose yourself to embody the qualities of the Source or Creator. During the incarnation meeting, your soul decided to pick certain challenges for you to awaken. And here you are reading this book trying to find God. Hence, you can say your soul's decision successfully brought you here. And you might not realize you have a plan to accomplish. Your soul decided this plan before incarnating, but you have completely forgotten your mission or plan due to the veil of forgetfulness. My job is for you to realize that you are here for a reason, and only you can help yourself to find your mission or plan. In the coming chapter, I will explain how to find out your mission or plan on Earth. But for now, let's focus on the incarnation process.

Let me explain further what goes into incarnation meetings and how different parameters are finalized. An incarnation meeting is held between the soul to be incarnated and two or more guides. The role of the guides is to help you by providing recommendations and suggestions for learning lessons that are needed to complete. Guides provide the soul with the environment it needs and different parameters that can help the soul fulfill its mission. The divine mission is decided by the soul and its guides, the mission's primary aim is soul graduation. Soul graduation is close to completing a set of tasks successfully by the soul for the soul to move to higher planetary realms. Earth is an environment that provides learning possibilities to souls to execute their tasks and, hence, move on to the next environment. Other planetary realms provide different environments and different parameters for learning. Coming back to Earth, Earth has been specifically designed and maintained so that souls can learn their lessons and successfully execute their tasks to graduate from Earth.

Let me give you a few examples of parameters: Separation from a loved one can either help the soul to expand and master the lesson of love, or the soul can derail from its path and choose to act in a manner harmful to other souls and self. The latter is not uncommon. This happens most of the time, but that does not mean the lesson is difficult. It means the soul needs multiple attempts to get it right and expand to align itself more with the Source. Hence, the lessons vary, like a chronic illness, the death of a loved one, or a challenging soul contract with a family member. These are all examples of how lessons can help the soul align better with the Source. I hope now you have clarity of why these lessons are important.

Let's return to the incarnation meeting after the soul decides the purpose and guides helping them design a life. A soul goes through its life and asks for a few changes to suit its journey of evolution. This is similar to a meeting on Earth where a product to be designed is carefully walked through with the product's user. All the possibilities of the product not working as expected are discussed, a few last-minute changes are added, and the product's success criteria are decided. Once the user is satisfied, the product is finalized and handed over to the user, which in this case is the soul. So a life, an incarnation on Earth, is handed over to the soul. I hope this example helps you understand the incarnation meeting. Do not take things literally since the difference between a product meeting and an incarnation meeting is huge when you consider the ultimate goal, the folks involved, and the divine purpose, which differs from product meetings where the ultimate goal is profits. However, the discussions around these two meetings regarding the designing part are similar.

Let's come to the second part, where the costume is handed over to the soul. This is an interesting process as well. Assume you are a fisherman and you want to catch fish. You put your fishing rod into the pond or lake and try to catch fish. Similarly, your soul uses an instrument to put a part of itself into the water, that is, the environment to be incarnated in. Now, here is the interesting part: Your soul is actually on the other side of the veil and uses an instrument to put a part of itself into the environment of Earth. Like the fishing rod explained in the example, your soul also has a grip on you. Your soul guides you from the other side of the veil, much like fishermen moving their fishing rod where they want. Whether you allow your soul to guide you is a different story.

Do not take the example literally. It's just a mechanism for your soul to incarnate its aspect on Earth. Most people have forgotten this connection with their soul. You are an incarnate aspect of your soul while your soul still rests on the other side of the veil with a connection to you, much like a fisherman holding his fishing rod underwater. You are on the other end of the fishing rod, which goes underwater, but you have forgotten that your soul is holding the rod and can guide you in your mission in this environment.

My purpose is to make you realize that you must use your soul's guidance. Your soul awaits your calling. You can ask your soul what next steps you should take in your life to fulfill your mission. The questions you can ask your soul can be as simple as whether you should drink coffee and what its effects are on your body or as complex as what next steps are associated with the soul mission you are supposed to execute. The communication between you and your soul can be words or non-linear communication. You will get answers as signals from your soul, like repetitively seeing something that you might think is a mere coincidence. Still, it might be nudges from your soul.

The nudges are not as simplistic as you may think. They vary from getting a nudge in a dream to meeting someone in your path multiple times. This makes you wonder if there is a purpose here. Nudges can be seeing something on TV or social media that might get you curious and make you ponder if it's aligned with your purpose. A nudge might be hearing a song where your soul might have something for you to focus on. Now you know the different channels your soul chooses for you to understand these nudges. Some of you consider these signs from the Universe. That will be accurate since it's your soul sitting on the other side of the veil, giving nudges through multiple channels for you to understand the steps you should take for your soul mission.

I hope this helps you understand your connection with your soul. This connection is purely divine and will always guide you toward what is best for you because it is your divine form guiding you in your earthly life. It's divine, sending you nudges and not a separate being telling you to take up your tasks. You need to consider this connection to be divine; only then will you be able to act on it and try to ask more questions to get clarity. Accept that you have a connection to the Creator because every soul is nothing but a fragment of the Creator.

The fragment of the Creator is the Creator itself, and being a fragment does not make it less than the Creator. This is a powerful statement because it helps you realize the creator in yourself and not as being a separate entity from you on Earth as a personality or a name. It is your soul, which is the Creator in itself, and so is the soul of everyone incarnated being on Earth. Hence, it makes everyone on Earth the Creator or God. God is sitting in you while you try to explore the world in search of God, asking people who think they have found the Creator in their version of a personality or a name. You only need to go within to find the Creator sitting inside of you with a connection to the other side of the veil, giving you nudges and signals to take up your soul mission. This understanding of the connection is the best gift you can give to yourself since acting on the signals will decide whether or not your life will be considered successful. And it's not easy to act on it sometimes because your soul might have tough decisions for you to take in the future. Your mind might resist or even reject the nudges and signals for you to stay in your comfort zone. After all, the mind likes to be in its comfort zone.

I hope this helps you understand the divine connection waiting to be heard by you to act on it. If you have found this connection and can understand its nudges and signals, your journey to find God is completed because you have found God within you.

Let's continue with why soul connection is the most important aspect of your life and why you can only fulfill your mission of this incarnation using this divine connection. Since your soul made plans to be incarnated on Earth for itself to evolve, it knows everything about your life, even at the minuscule level. Hence, this connection can be used to ask your soul what its soul mission is and what steps you should take. This divine connection will guide you in ways you cannot imagine. Think about a constant telephone connection to God where you can call and ask questions anytime. It is much like that, in this case, quite literally. You can ask your soul anything and everything. Do not ever feel that you may be asking too many questions. Your soul has all the time in the world to answer. Hence, make full use of this connection to the divine.

Let us learn how to activate this connection and know whether you are talking to your soul. Since you are reading this book, I would say you are in communication with your soul because your soul directed you here, and you listened to your soul and started reading this book. Soul communication is not something that can be generalized like I am talking to you now with this book. Similarly, the soul has various channels to speak to you, varying from direct communication using thoughts, that is, hearing a voice within you guiding you or contacting channelers who can help you provide information from your soul and the ways I explained earlier.

Let us come to what you can ask your soul and how exactly you make your soul answer your queries. Your soul cannot give all the information of the pre-incarnation meeting to you during your incarnation. Your soul can only point you toward the direction or steps you seek at a given moment. The trick is to ask questions in a way that shows you the next steps in the here and now, a yes or no for a particular action to be taken. That way, your soul can guide you to a conclusion. If you want to know your soul mission, you can ask your soul whether you have agreed to do something particular or not. However, your soul will never hand you the entire map of your incarnation all at once. There is a difference between seeking guidance and asking the whole thing from your soul. You have to practice seeking guidance and confirmation for things you came to or want to come to a conclusion about. I hope my advice makes it clearer how to ask your soul questions.

LESSON 4: SOUL MISSION AND ITS ALIGNMENT WITH THE MISSION OF EARTH

Let us focus on how your soul mission fits together with the planetary mission, what you accomplish by acting on your soul mission, and what it means for Earth.

Earth was a beautiful planet where so many kingdoms lived together in harmony; that was the case during Atlantis – Earth's Golden Age. But since the fall of Atlantis, many things have gone wrong, especially the actions of humanity, which have made this planet inhabitable for other kingdoms, plants, minerals, and animals. The actions of humanity have destroyed a great heritage of Earth. This destruction cannot be recovered in a day; it requires commitment and dedication of incarnated aspects of souls for Earth to replenish and serve as a good host for all kingdoms.

Earth was not what you see today. Earth had beautiful skies, vegetation, scenery that left humans' minds in awe, and beauty beyond humanity's imagination. This beautiful planet was once home to many beings who came from other galaxies to learn and evolve as part of the curriculum of Earth. Many souls have had their classes on Earth and had a wonderful time learning. You can't even imagine souls from different parts of the galaxy coming to Earth to learn; this seems very far due to the actions of humanity.

First, humanity started exploiting trees as well as the natural habitat of nature beings, which resulted in the leaving of nature beings in parts of the world that are not visible to humanity. These nature beings tried their best to work alongside humanity but gave up once they saw humanity's destructive actions. With their head down, they left humanity alone in their journey; humanity was left with nothing but themselves to rely on and settle their population within their understanding of nature and requirements. With a lack of knowledge, humanity took steps that led them even further into darkness, and this darkness was even more difficult for us to help humanity get out of it.

We sent a few souls to incarnate on Earth to protect and maintain the current natural habitat but to no avail. They failed their missions since humanity as a collective did not listen to them and did not allow any of them to modify their existing way of living and destruction. I am sure you all know what I am talking about. At this stage, humanity is at least aware of the destruction they are doing thanks to incarnated aspects who took among themselves to fight the oppressors and take down systems that were harmful to everyone living on Earth, including the human population.

Our goal is not just to make humanity aware but to take down these systems that are wreaking havoc on our planet. The consequences of human actions are disruptive to our planet beyond measure. The necessary change must come from the incarnated aspects of souls who have agreed to undertake missions to preserve and help the planet. Their missions are not ordinary ones. Their mission is to take down empires that are causing nothing but destruction. I do not mean to scare you or pressure you. I ask you to imagine taking down big corporations who have destroyed our planet, causing harm to other kingdoms to such a great extent that it will take decades for them to trust us again to work with us harmoniously. Some of you reading this book have taken such gigantic soul missions to take down the systems of exploitation and destruction and rehabilitate Earth again with your strategy and guidance from us at Shambala. We are waiting for you to ask us how Earth can replenish again. Do not feel pressured since you have done this kind of work before and were chosen for this job. You have it in your genes to fight for the future of our planet, including but not limited to making people aware of their actions and how it affects our planet as a whole.

Only you can help Earth grow healthy again. Without you taking your soul missions seriously, Earth will be lost once more. And this time, there would be no comeback possible. I hope my words have stirred your emotions and a soulful longing to do what it takes for Mother Earth and its preservation. You will have all our support from Shambala. We are waiting for you to take on tasks that you agreed on before incarnating on Earth. You do not remember, but you agreed, along with many, to do whatever it takes to help other kingdoms trust humanity again, like during the time of Atlantis.

Each of your soul missions is unique and aligns with soul missions undertaken by other incarnated aspects. Your soul mission will help other incarnated aspects build upon it to fulfill their own soul missions. Their souls are waiting for you to take up your soul mission and start working towards it. There is a connection with thousands of soul missions that your mind is not completely able to comprehend. Trust us when we say that after you take your soul mission seriously, incarnated aspects of souls will turn to you in huge numbers. This has been planned and in the works for a long time now. Your soul mission has the power to unlock the soul missions of thousands, maybe millions of souls who have volunteered to help Earth revive. Ask yourself this question: Will my contribution help other souls? Of course, it will because all are interconnected. Hence, start working towards it since the future mission work of many others depends on you taking your mission seriously.

Do not let your ego mind persuade you otherwise since the mind loves comfort and comfort zones. Instead, think of what you can achieve for Earth and other kingdoms. Future generations will be thankful to you that you took your mission seriously and acted upon your soul's guidance. I hope this perspective will help you open your heart to take your soul mission seriously, serving Earth like you agreed before incarnating.

A soul mission is a complex set of tasks the soul and spirit guides decide. Usually, a soul mission involves a big mission for Earth and a mission toward self-development. Normally, both of these missions are interlinked in that the soul first needs lessons for self-development to then be of service to Earth. Your mission in this incarnation would also involve a self-development mission and a mission in service of planet Earth. I am sure you have gone through at least a few if not all, self-development lessons that anchored you to become a better version of yourself and be of service to Earth. Sometimes, there are collective missions where a few incarnated aspects of souls need to go through similar challenges, which help them become stronger and grow as a community to serve Earth. Most of you will form a community with people your soul agreed to be part of to contribute towards Earth's healing by working together as part of that community.

Community missions are more likely to be successful than individual soul missions. Imagine a heavy load being lifted by four to five people; there are different ways these people can distribute their part in lifting the heavy load. It can happen either by taking turns lifting it or by more mature souls lifting the heavier part of the load for the others to benefit. A group can adapt according to the group mission, but an individual cannot hold a heavy load alone for long. A breakdown will be necessary for the individual if the load becomes unbearable. And that is why our message is to work together in groups even if individual soul missions have little alignment. Do not try to be a lone warrior; you will become tired of fighting alone. Find people who think like you. Reach out to them if necessary, and work together to accomplish your respective soul missions. I would advise working with at least two to five people who have a soul mission similar to yours and can work together with you to fulfill individual soul missions as a collective one.

This advice would be helpful for long-term missions where you need determination and faith in your soul mission. We realize that for a few, it might be tough since your soul mission is unique, and others cannot help much. As for those, reach out to people you trust and form a community to seek constant guidance. Those people can play an indirect role in your soul mission even if they cannot share the load with you directly. This is powerful advice. Keep it in mind because you do not know when the load might get too heavy for you to bear, and you might need support. You now realize the importance of community and people coming together for critical soul missions to share the load and make it easier on individuals. I will end this chapter by explaining the importance of not giving up on your soul mission.

Importance of not giving up on your soul mission

A soul mission, as complex or serious as this term sounds to you, is just a set of tasks to be accomplished on Earth. You may not realize if you unknowingly completed certain tasks of your soul mission. On Earth, these tasks are similar to any other tasks that need to be done by an incarnated aspect of a soul. There is nothing that makes these tasks special but just the willingness of your soul to accomplish them.

You might have made a serious commitment in your mind of your soul mission being difficult. But you need to realize that, like any other task you accomplish on Earth, a soul mission has a similar set of tasks. Before becoming aware of your soul mission, you thought of living a normal life of working at a corporation or a business, getting married, having kids, retiring one day, and spending time with your family. And you may not realize that this can be a soul mission for a few, but for most, it might be other things. My point is, do not feel pressure to accomplish your soul mission; pressure makes it difficult. Consider your soul mission just like any other task on Earth that your soul has opted to accomplish. Labeling a simple task as a soul mission does not make it difficult; it might be difficult in your mind, but the difficulty remains whether or not you consider it your soul mission.

Soul missions are decided purely on the calibre of the soul, that is, how much a soul can contribute and is willing to contribute. Everyone's calibre is known at Shambala. You have been given exactly the type of mission you are capable of implementing. Your capability can be seen by us, not by you in the dense physical of Earth. We can help you access it. Your capabilities lie dormant, waiting for you to get activated and come to the surface. We know how you can align to your capabilities, but first, you must trust us. Nothing can be achieved without trust; it is the prime ingredient of difficult soul missions.

The difficulty of soul missions is a carefully calculated variable that we use to compare here at Shambala. Clearly, looking at soul mission difficulty varies from easy to difficult to most difficult. Difficult to most difficult soul missions are reserved for very mature souls, which are souls who have demonstrated their capabilities in previous incarnations and lived up to their tasks. These soul missions have a separate team, an advanced team. The advanced team carefully designs their soul mission. Few of you reading this book have an advanced team with you. With an advanced team, you get more perks, meaning: guidance from the most advanced souls on this planet, along with nudges given to you in a more elaborate way than usual. These nudges are like direct signals letting the incarnate aspect of a soul know that it is supposed to take the next steps.

Most of you reading this book have received nudges. Some understand while some do not, and there are many who, even after understanding the nudges, refrain from taking action. The reason behind this is a lack of trust. Trust is the most important thing when it comes to difficult soul missions. The difficulty is easily overcome if there is trust. Having great trust in your guides and us equals great soul mission execution. You may think that in order to accomplish your soul mission, the most important thing is acting on it, but from our perspective, it is trust.

Acting without trust is not a great step. The steps you take without trust may have no foundation, and you merely do what is asked by your soul and guides. This type of action does not hold good in the long term. It can wither away in the short term. The trust should be so immense that you trust nobody more on Earth. It requires surrender that your team of guides has got your back no matter what. It is this knowing that whatever happens is fine and will work out in the long term; it is very simple.

The conditioning on Earth makes you doubt everything: Will it work or not? Can I achieve this? Or worse, am I even the right person to do it? These doubts arise from conditioning on Earth. Things work out at the end, especially when your guides say so. This was my way of helping you all take the leap and trust. Trust us with your life that we have got your back. What more would you need? This is the highest we can offer from this side of the veil and occasional help with material things for genuine reasons that ultimately lead to good. This is all we have to offer, and we try our best, but taking the leap of faith is in your control.

We expect you all to talk to your soul and us for guidance and the next steps. Your soul mission is the hope of Earth. Without your soul missions, hope is lost, and so are we; we rely on you all to take the leap. It may be ordinary for you in the dense physical, and not many people will give you recognition, but we will. Our team of guides and your support team, we will celebrate you every day, even for the tiny steps you take, as they will have a major impact on the collective from our perspective. We see it clearly.

LESSON 5: THE NEW AGE AND HOW WILL IT LOOK LIKE

The golden period would be new to many, and first, it is important to understand how things will work in the New Age. You have seen the system of old, which operates on separation, greed, self-service, and very little thinking about the collective. The separation exists from the micro to the macro level, and it's important to address it for the New Age. But first, let me give you a glimpse of the coming New Age—a state of pure bliss and love. Love is the highlight of the New Age. Care for each and every fellow human being, care for Mother Nature, and care for other kingdoms. Care will come from the inherent understanding that we are one, living as different souls that belong together in Unity and will merge back into the Source as one. The realization of this truth and acceptance of it is the prerequisite for you to enter the New Age.

Our Earth, our Gaia, hosts many kingdoms and beings, and many of them will be new to you in the coming of the New Age. These beings, however different, are similar to us. They want to unite with us for our and their evolutionary journey.

These beings vary from devas, dragons, unicorns, centaurs, phoenixes, fairies to many more you have never heard of. The Earth belongs to them as much as it does to human beings. The first step would be trusting them, accepting them as our own, and interacting with them. Once you start interacting with them, you will realize how similar they are to you. That being said, in the New Age, we all will see these beings clearly; yes, it would be as easy as that. You can see them right now with your etheric vision if your third eye is open. Many people have advanced in their spiritual journey enough that they can talk to and see these beings easily, but they have had special training or come with their own soul gifts, which makes it easier. If you want to start seeing these beings now, start your spiritual training and find different ways to open your third eye. It is not as complex as you may think. With our support, it can happen in a few days, along with certain training.

Training is like a small curriculum where you understand what you already see or hear. Many of you do not realize yet that you do talk to a lot of higher divine beings. The voice in your head might give you a certain suggestion, and you may think it is your own mind, but it is not always the case. We do talk to a lot of you quite regularly, and it's just the realization that you are talking to us where training is needed.

Conversing with us is like conversing with a friend; you ask a question or share your opinion, and we offer our thoughts to you. However, you need to be attentive to our thoughts; you cannot just ask a question and then forget about the conversation. You have to be open to us, to your soul, and allow some time to listen with curiosity. If you are asking questions into darkness, not expecting a response, you will not hear a response, even if we provide one. We understand this process might be difficult for some, but the fruits are priceless. What you can achieve for yourself and Earth is unmeasurable. With the activation of this communication as well as proper training and guidance, you can move mountains.

You also have to understand that we devise tasks for humanity, and we have a much wider perspective. We can see and understand the current state of Earth at a larger scale with many details. With that, we design these tasks to be taken up by you. Once you understand the task, you can ask as many questions as you want, but the task cannot be changed. You can leave the task anytime you want, but you cannot change the expectations of the task. It is meant to be fulfilled in a certain way and in a certain pattern. We have a lot of experience and therefore advise you to take certain steps. If you are not comfortable with a task, you may negotiate part of it, yet you cannot change the entire way of executing it. It is with very detailed and careful discussions that we have designed these tasks, and they are not to be taken lightly.

You were chosen because you have potential for it and not because you were our only option. We have many options when we decide what tasks need to be accomplished by whom. Many thorough and detailed discussions by very experienced and wise souls take place for this purpose. When the assignment is executed, you have to be carefree about it and your ability to fulfill it. If you have a strong sense of determination, you will be able to fulfill it no matter what, but we need your determination and commitment. Without it, we cannot help you. We have seen you exhibit these characteristics, and that is why we want to work with you. Have faith in us. Once we choose you, you have the full potential to fulfill and execute the task perfectly. Your self-doubt comes from a place of history of what you have tried in the past, and you have had a few disappointments in your life that made you think about whether you are good enough. It's different for your new tasks: Now you have the will of Source with you, divine support, and support by many you cannot see or sense yet. That being said, it is important for you to act as if you will execute your task perfectly. There is no reason to doubt yourself.

People and the cities

Atlantis had many cities around the world; it was a huge continent with more than 500 cities and 200 villages. It certainly was a prime time for Earth and its inhabitants. Atlantis hosted beings from different galaxies and our galaxy as guests. Atlantis had many big cities like the ones we have now and also very big buildings, bigger than the biggest buildings on Earth right now. You can imagine the advancement of humanity during this time. It was certainly the best time seen so far by Earth and its inhabitants.

Compared to Atlantis, the current time period feels like we

have gone back to being cavemen. I use this comparison carefully to make you understand that the current development of humanity is at the primal stage, which needs a leap of evolution to go back to its Golden Age. This cannot be achieved unless there is a spiritual leap of evolution completed. Humanity needs to undergo this leap with us being their guides, along with galactic beings who are here to assist. The event will happen sooner than people think. For us, it has already happened, and we are looking at the future civilization of humanity growing and flowering in the Golden Age.

This period humanity is going through can be considered the pre-Atlantic period since we have not reached the Golden Age yet, while we are almost out of the old systems. We are in the middle right now, with new energies coming to Earth and filling the entire civilization with positive energies, thereby anchoring a great change in humanity's thought process and their entire being to match that of the Golden Age. This process started in 2012 and will be completed by 2032, taking many to a level of transformation they cannot comprehend right now. Humanity is prepared to go through certain shocks of their life because, in the next few years, they will see and witness things their history does not have details about. Humanity will try to make sense of it by going back to ancient scriptures, but it will be of no help since this event has never happened on Earth before. Scriptures cannot help you there; only prophecies made by a few spiritually advanced communities will be able to justify these events accurately.

My purpose with this book is for people to understand that the coming of the New Age does not need to be understood logically. Just try to accept it, and it will be beneficial for your soul and you. Trying to fight it, clinging to old systems, will be a disappointment for your soul. Your soul planned this incarnation for you to graduate rather than cling to old systems and outdated constructs of society. Moving on with your new life will be a wise thing to do, which your soul desperately is waiting for you to do.

LESSON 6: ATLANTIS AND ITS KINGDOMS

Spirituality was the foundation of Atlantis. Everyone knew the truth of God, and it was common knowledge. Rarely were there any who did not have advanced spiritual knowledge of the cosmos. The spiritual truth of self-realization, the God within, and we as fragments of God was as common as knowing how to walk. You will be surprised how spiritually advanced humanity was during Atlantis. Instant manifestation was common as well. There was no financial system to keep people locked into dependency and work for others for survival. People in Atlantis worked only for common goals, together in unity, and rarely were there communities in conflict. Even if a conflict arose, it was handled by spiritually advanced beings, and everyone trusted them no matter what. There was no hidden agenda of any being. If you needed something, especially for day-to-day needs, you could manifest it out of thin air. It was that simple.

I understand this sounds very enticing, and today humanity needs a lot of help and support to get there. It will not be easy. With so many people fighting against spirituality and oneness, it is a humongous task. Even people who are spiritually inclined stick to old scriptures that were true at that time, justifying deeds of today by scriptures written thousands of years ago by humans just like you and me. The reason old scriptures are given more importance is that they seem more trustworthy as compared to people who might have hidden agendas. Because of trust issues, people usually fall back to the scriptures. Some think that without them, they are lost.

Scriptures are helpful when they support your spiritual development, but sometimes scriptures can cause harm and not give you a wider perspective of how things work unless you do go in-depth and pursue further. It is time now to let go of old systems and scriptures to enter into the Golden Age awaiting us. Your soul knows what's best for you. Communicating with your soul will help you understand this. The Bhagavad Gita holds a lot of truth today as well, but you need to realize that when Krishna imparted this knowledge, humanity was in a dark age where Krishna tried his best to impart the knowledge needed for humanity to advance spiritually.

I, MAITREYA, was Krishna. I was there during the time of Mahabharata when Arjuna needed to hear spiritual truth desperately. I was the one who imparted verses to Arjuna, which you call Bhagavad Gita. During the time of recitation, I did not name it, but it was Vyasa who named it Bhagavad Gita and published it in Sanskrit for humanity. It has served for thousands of years till now and helped people understand spiritual truth. Even today, you can use Bhagavad Gita to advance spiritually if you take my words in the book seriously. It is still considered an immense book of knowledge by us in Shambala.

I was Krishna, and you are Krishna as well. I am within you, and you are within me. We all are one, one true God. I wanted humanity to understand this with my teachings. I wanted everyone who read the Bhagavad Gita to understand that there is no separation between God and human beings. Each and every human being is God. Just like you are having a human experience on Earth, I was a human being too. I never said that only I am God, and the rest is not. You are with me as there is one God which exists in all of us. You have forgotten due to the laws of Earth but soon will remember it when the Golden Age comes back to Earth. I am now back to impart my teachings to humanity for this leap of evolution.

My coming will make many uncomfortable, and they will try to find flaws, putting a lot of logic in things, going back to ancient scriptures where they will try to find some or the other thing which will make them justify the thoughts they have already decided in their mind. I want to say I understand your point of view, and I do not blame you for not accepting it completely because this is what conditioning has done to humanity. From childhood, a certain way of thinking is allowed, and a lot of caution is installed in children not to believe everything they hear or see. To all those people, I say: ask your soul! Your soul knows the answer. Your mind may come in between with logic and quotes from ancient scriptures, but your soul already understands the truth, the truth of the impending coming of the Golden Age. I hope you start talking to your soul on a daily basis to understand what to trust and what to let go.

Communicating with your soul is what I, along with others, teach at NAMAS YOUNIVERSITY, a digital university guiding people to activate their gifts and initiate communication with their souls. I, along with The SANAT KUMARA, YESHUA (JESUS), MOTHER MARY, and SAINT GERMAIN, speak about the spiritual guidance you all need during this time to make the spiritual leap.

At NAMAS YOUNIVERSITY, our goal is for twenty-five percent of humanity to reach soul guidance along with Shambala guidance in the next three to four decades. This will be achieved in phases where, initially, people will graduate to the fifth dimension and then achieve soul guidance. The plan for humanity is first to understand the meaning of soul guidance, the intent behind the provision of soul guidance by your soul, and how you can achieve your soul mission with the help of your soul's guidance.

Soul guidance is like a fruit with sweet and nutritious contents waiting for you to be opened up and accessed for your own good and development. As soul guidance may sometimes mean uncomfortable decisions to take, understanding that there is a higher purpose behind it is essential for each of you.

Guidance may sometimes make you feel uncomfortable, and that is absolutely fine since your soul's will is waiting for you to accept and act on it. It is not that difficult. Connecting to your soul and listening curiously will help you get the answers you are looking for.

NAMAS YOUNIVERSITY's mission is to activate those twenty-five percent of the human population with soul guidance. But first, let us come to the purpose of NAMAS YOUNIVERSITY. The purpose is to make human beings aware of their forgotten true nature, access their multidimensional self, and understand different life forms on Earth. Different life forms are deva beings, the plants and mineral kingdom, the Conree and Oblan kingdom, and the animal kingdom. These kingdoms hold the same importance as humanity on Earth. It is important for humanity to live harmoniously and work together with them. First, please realize the importance of each of these kingdoms. It is like meeting your brothers and sisters. The five kingdoms of Earth represent oneness.

How these five kingdoms lived in Atlantis

It was not long ago when these five kingdoms of Earth mingled with each other like friends from different neighborhoods. Some held a closer bond than with their own kind; it was beautiful. Human beings and devas especially were very close to each other, like two neighboring countries having excellent relationships with each other. There were no boundaries and rules stopping them from meeting each other. Devas helped humanity by explaining to them how their own body works and functions, much like today's doctors who explain human anatomy. Modern-day doctors have just scratched the surface. Today's doctors have discovered a lot of things, but still, they do not have any idea how the human body interacts with different energies. They ignore that the human body itself is a form of energy interacting with surroundings, the energy that gives form to the incarnated aspect of the soul.

The human body is like the soul's temple, a temporary station that helps the soul provide an environment to face challenges and experiences it can gather and master to move closer to the Source. Devas are very innocent beings who can help humanity understand itself, and humanity can help devas by providing a platform for growth in order to master their own lessons as deva beings. Humans provide a perspective to deva beings of how the bodies they designed help humans achieve their soul mission. Devas are counterparts of humans; they complement each other.

Devas create all physical and etheric life forms for souls to get encapsulated and live as life forms on Earth. Animals, fish, and plants are all made by devas. Without devas, there would be no physical life form in this universe and souls to learn and experience such ways for their own evolution. The physicality of your being, from the tiniest element in your body to different organs and body parts, everything is designed by deva beings. They are the architects of the world.

Deva beings are responsible for providing you with a child's body during birth and making changes to it with time. You think everything happens automatically, but that is not true. Devas take care of your body during your incarnation. They look out for you and make modifications if needed. Devas create a blueprint for your body and for how it will change during your incarnation. Your soul gives devas input on how it wants to experience its life and if there are any challenges the soul needs to master. Devas make a note of all the things that your soul wants to experience and start building a life form to sustain you on Earth and a temporary station for an aspect of your soul to enter and act like a life form during the incarnation.

Devas and human souls work together during the soul's incarnation and make modifications to the plan if needed for the soul family or soul community. Humans provide their perspective and feedback to devas regarding the soul's journey for devas to improve their process; it's a mutual relationship with both having each of their roles to fulfill.

The Source has divinely planned these roles, and the souls have chosen their path of evolution towards the Source. Source creates a plan for each and every one. This means that there exists a divine plan for humanity and devas. This plan states that devas and humans are supposed to work together and evolve together until they become one. The human family is one, and the deva family is one. Together, they form a family.

The human family was once very close to their deva counterparts, and devas used to help humanity during the time of Atlantis. Humanity served devas as well. Atlantis had many kingdoms, with each kingdom having its leaders and communities. Humans had their representatives, and devas had their representatives. Humans built technology faster than they should have, ridiculed deva counterparts and considered themselves to be above devas, which eventually led to the downfall. Since then, there have been multiple attempts to bring humans and devas closer again, but in vain.

During the current time of ascension, the union of these two groups is inevitable. Atlantis will reemerge. Deva beings are waiting for human beings to take the leap and work together with them in close association. Some might even turn out to be your best friends from past lives. During Atlantis and Lemuria, association with devas was common knowledge, and all were aware of the divine plan. The plan had a lot of details. First and foremost, how are humans and Devas supposed to work together?

Both have an equal role. Humans have a role in evolving with the help of devas since devas build their life forms on the physical and etheric planes. Devas understand human requirements and provide a life form for each and every human soul. Similarly, humans provide devas the opportunity to evolve by being an anchor of their role. Humans help devas understand and fulfill the evolutionary requirements needed by individual souls. Humans provide devas with an opportunity to be an architect of their life form and improve on the details. Humans are recipients of the vessel created by devas and hence act as a learning catalyst for devas to improve on their creation skills as architects of life forms on Earth. This learning catalyzation helps devas evolve and provide opportunities for growth, just like humans. Creation is the devas' way of existence. Maintaining the creation and decomposition of the creation is part of the devas' evolutionary journey.

Devas create by using the help of elementals. Elementals have their own evolutionary journey on the path of creation of life forms. Elementals are devas at the primary level. They evolve and become deva beings in charge of creating whole bodies, communities, and later entire civilizations along with the planet. Elementals are single-purpose life forms that work on specific tasks they can perform. An individual deva being works with elementals their whole life to create and maintain life forms. Elementals are an integral part of humanity's evolution; acknowledging them and working with them would be the first step.

Elves

Elves were devas once; they voluntarily chose to modify their being in order to be protected from humans. Humans exploited devas with their invocations and tried to enslave them for their own needs. Some devas, along with others, came to an agreement that devas were not safe and needed protection from humans. In order to be protected from human invocations, devas collectively agreed to add an extra chakra to their being, which helped them protect themselves. These newly created beings were the elves. Elves then separated from the devas and created their own kingdom. Separation among devas was created as well. Since the fall of Atlantis, devas and elves lived in separation until 2021, when these kingdoms merged into one, signifying the unity among them. They are waiting for humans to unite, which will happen soon in the near future. Devas and elves now work together with their tasks and display no separation between them. They are also meant to assist humanity in their evolutionary journey.

Since the fall of Atlantis, elves have lived alone, in separation from Shambala. After unification, the kingdom of elves now works with the SANAT KUMARA and Shambala to bring back Earth to its divine plan. Earth is changing its energies every second of every day. The energies emanating from Earth now are filled with high frequencies of the New Earth. The change is already happening for a few of you, and you are now able to talk to your higher self or soul and hear voices every now and then. These voices guide you, but you have to listen and trust them in order for you to enter New Earth. It has already been created and is waiting for you to enter and live there. We are waiting for you there as well.

LESSON 7: SPIRITUAL GROWTH DURING THIS PERIOD OF ASCENSION

Dear readers, the previous chapters focused on soul lessons, incarnation plans, and opportunities for soul growth. In this chapter, I will focus on what spiritual growth is needed for you to be eligible for this shift or ascension.

Like any other facet of your life, spiritual growth requires consistent work, dedication, and commitment. It cannot happen by simply letting things happen in your life. You must be in the driver's seat, taking control of your life. I will revisit this important aspect later. Spiritual growth is a series of lessons that the incarnated aspect consciously agrees to go through. For example, you may decide to discontinue working at an unfulfilling job that is not serving you any purpose other than money.

We realize money is important to survive on Earth, but first, you must be true to yourself. Are you earning money for your survival or to fit into society? Can you do with less money? Money has played a huge role in many people's lives, stopping their spiritual growth. Spiritual growth requires you to let go of old patterns and societal conditioning. You can find income that would be enough for yourself and focus on spiritual growth during this incarnation, where earning does not make you feel pressured but comes naturally.

Income is one of the aspects we can help you with if you choose to work with us. But since most of you would need income until the New Age arises, I would advise letting go of the income source where you are earning to fit into society and finding a job or business that aligns with your spiritual principles. What do I mean by spiritual principles? It means work that aligns with Earth's divine plan. This can include helping people understand and making them aware of actions of humans that can mold or destroy Earth's future, providing healing services to people who need them during this period, providing spiritual material to help people evolve their understanding, or providing any tools which people can use to evolve further on their path. Your services should help Earth, humanity, and all kingdoms living on Earth. When your job or business aligns with these principles, it will help you evolve further on your spiritual journey, no matter where you are on your journey.

Now, since I have covered the income aspect, let us come to the family aspect. Many ambassadors of light are dimming their light in order to fit into their family and group of friends; this is as bad as not awakening at all. If you have awakened, your job is to awaken others; it should not be the other way around. Awakening is a gift that your soul has planned to occur at a certain point in your life. This gift should be used wisely and for the benefit of people. Adjusting oneself to fit into society is a gift wasted. If you are certain that people around you will not awaken, for example, your family and friends, then it is time to leave their company because you may not realize that gradually you will be dimming your light on a daily basis in order to be in their company and at later point completely forget about your spiritual mission.

This has happened with many awakened souls, and the primary reason they are not coming forward is because they cannot let go of their family and friends with whom they no longer resonate. If you are reading this book, I am sure your awakening has already started or is in the initial stages. I want to convey with this lesson that awakening is not something to be taken lightly. You have awakened to your true self; this does not happen often on Earth. Make full use of it, even if that means taking tough calls or letting go of old friends and family members who are not getting awakened with your help. It is time to let go once you are certain that they will not awaken.

During this period, you will meet many people like you on

their spiritual journey. It will happen sooner or later. You will meet your soul family and form new friendships along the way, which will help you nurture the relationships again. It is not a lonely journey; only you can make it lonely if you decide not to meet new people. But if you are open-minded and open-hearted, you will form soul-level friendships you will cherish for the rest of your life on Earth.

I want to add that after making tough calls, you may have certain moments where you may think of returning to the old life. These moments test if, indeed, you are a match for the New Earth. You must have faith, faith in your soul guidance, spirit guides, and us. Faith is a powerful vibration. Leaving everything to divine powers during this period will help you stay on your spiritual path. It is not easy to walk down this path, but it is truly fulfilling for your soul once you realize how many lives are affected by one simple act toward the foundations of the New Earth. It creates a ripple effect that can affect millions of people to awaken to their true selves. Just think of small acts and how powerful they are for people on Earth.

Now, let me cover other aspects of spiritual growth. First and foremost is the realization of the true self; it's a heavy term, but what exactly does it mean? It means that when you know, you are not a human but a fragment of a much bigger divine power manifested in your body as a human. What is that divine power? It is your soul. Your soul is you, the real you, and not the human aspect. Your soul has sent a small aspect of itself into a body. This aspect in itself is a divine essence. The divine essence in you comes from the qualities already present in your soul. You and your soul have the same divine qualities; hence, the qualities that you observe in day-to-day life actually come from your soul. Your soul has manifested these qualities in a human vehicle, but these qualities are only a fraction of what your soul chose to manifest in you, i.e., the human aspect of your soul that is due to lessons and your soul mission.

For example, the qualities of helping others, donating money to those in need, appreciating people, nurturing others, or as simple qualities as being polite and calm during tough times, and many other divine qualities. These are all divine qualities of your soul manifested in you. Now you know why certain people are kinder than others, more helping or nurturing than others.

Just because a person demonstrates these qualities does not necessarily mean that their soul had them; these can also be developed in an incarnation due to environmental factors or challenges the incarnate aspect went through to embody those qualities.

Spiritual growth during this period of the Shift is necessary for your soul to graduate to the New Earth. Just making yourself aware of the process of ascension is not enough. You may know a lot of details of the process but still have a lot of spiritual baggage to deal with. For spiritual growth, a lot of discipline and practice of spirituality is needed. You need to understand that only actual spiritual growth ensures your ascension rather than mere knowledge about spirituality. Actual work needs to be done by you, like harmonizing your ego-mind, being mentally tough, letting go of old harmful behavioral patterns, and letting go of limiting beliefs that do not serve you. All this is needed to ascend. It is not merely a process of getting to know about ascension but actually implementing it.

Some are going through tough lessons, and some have already mastered a lot of their lessons. Hence, they will be the first ones to ascend. It is not about priority, though. There is no bias in this process. It is all about spiritual growth. That growth is completely in your hands. We can guide you, help you, and give you resources, but we cannot take the leap for you toward your spiritual growth. It is completely voluntary and available to all.

You may choose to evolve spiritually during this time or not, and that will decide whether you get to be part of New Earth. Some may think this is a harsh process, but the New Earth demands these qualities from you. Understanding your mind and its intricacies will be the first step, and then harmonizing all your desires, urges, and thoughts of low vibration. These all need to be harmonized and released. Eventually, you will learn not to act on them because you understand the games of the mind.

The process, however tough, is fair to all, and it is easier than you may think. Evolving spiritually is all about letting go of old customs and conditioning, constructs of blood family relations, understanding and adapting the constructs of your soul family, and mastering abilities like telepathy, channeling, and others.

Some may have these questions: If you do not let go of the old but still act on soul guidance, will you be able to ascend? To answer this question, I first need you to understand what soul guidance is. When you are acting on your soul's guidance, you will take steps to let go of the old as your soul yearns for it. Acting on soul guidance is nothing but evolving spiritually. Let me give you an example: Consider a spiritually inclined person making decisions on their own, not realizing the importance of soul guidance, but the person has some experience with soul guidance and chooses to ignore it. It will not help the person evolve spiritually if he or she does not act on guidance given by the soul.

Receiving guidance but not acting on it may block your ascension to the New Earth. Acting is as important as receiving. You may not always like what you receive, but you need to trust; and trust that it is in your best interest to act on it. Only by acting on what you receive from your soul can you evolve spiritually. There may be decisions you do not understand or even resist, but only your soul knows the importance of that decision. You may even get details as to why your soul needs you to take that step. Whether or not your soul tells you the reason why, you should still act on the decision your soul needs you to take. Trusting that your soul knows better than you is crucial. Your life in the dense physical might be affected by the decision big time, but your soul yearns for you to take that decision. Realize the importance of soul guidance and acting on it.

Importance of Spirituality in day-to-day life

Before starting with this section, I assume that you have at least some idea about your soul mission. If not, I would strongly suggest you find out and start acting on it. Spirituality has been a separate subject for many years. People take an interest in it at their convenience; some treat it as a hobby, and some use it for discussion purposes.

The purpose of spirituality has been limited on Earth for thousands of years; you must have observed it in your family, with friends or other people surrounding you. You might have more inclination towards spirituality than others, and although it is beautiful to learn about spirituality, it is more important to go into deeper self-realization. Self-realization may seem difficult to you on Earth because that is the idea installed in your head by external conditioning. The idea of self-realization is the mere truth of knowing your true self. This idea may seem abstract to some because they have heard this multiple times and do not know how to do it. Others may have embarked on their journey of finding their true self with no luck.

Knowing is a simple process, like how you know it's day or night during any given time of the day. Similarly, knowing your true self is not a complicated, difficult process. You just know it.

How do you know if you know the truth of self-realization? It's a discovery, but one thing is important – you should know where to look and where to go, whom to ask and whom to trust. You will get thousands of answers from enlightened people or people who think they are enlightened. A lot of times, the information you receive will be contradictory and will confuse you further about whom to believe and trust. This process is tough but necessary. Once you know whom to believe, you have at least chosen a path, a right or wrong path; that time will tell. Making choices is necessary because until and unless you do not choose, you will not know whether or not it is for you. You cannot judge and make decisions from the outside. Even a wrong choice will help you learn where not to go and what does not align with your soul.

Your true self is your entire being, not just the human part that you can see and feel. Your entire being includes those parts you cannot see or feel. The knowing that your being encompasses those parts as well does not necessarily come from your sensory organs. Your soul can detect any parts of you that you cannot detect with your senses. Let me explain in more depth:

You cannot detect your true self, and for a good reason, but that does not mean it is not you. It just means that on a physical level, there is no provision for you to feel and make sense of it. On the physical plane, you are just a mind with limited thoughts, but on the spiritual level, you are so much more than that. It is crucial for you to understand on the physical plane that it is not important for you to feel or sense your entire true being. Simply know that it exists!

DEVA OF HUMANITY

Now that you all know who devas are and what their job is, I want to cover in brief 'The Deva Of Humanity.' Not long ago, humanity lived peacefully along with other kingdoms as a family. Amnesia was not present in humans at that time, and they had complete knowledge about their role in the cosmos. During this time there was a powerful being helping us maintain balance with other kingdoms. The Deva Of Humanity was helping humanity build a good relationship with devas and keeping the balance between them. The role of the Deva of Humanity was to serve both kingdoms as a human liaison for devas. It was a critical and important position. The Deva of Humanity was a renowned personality of Earth, and they considered all humans their children. It was no ordinary position; it came with many great responsibilities towards humans and devas. The position was synonymous with the Chief Relationship Officer of the kingdoms, acting as an intermediary to have both kingdoms evolve with each other. The Deva of Humanity lived among us before the fall of Atlantis, like a happy parent peacefully living with its children. When Atlantis fell, the Deva of Humanity lost its children and had to go under deep sleep until the time was right for rebirth. The Deva of Humanity waited a long time to work with humans and tried her best to be there for humans after the fall but with deep sorrow, she had to go under deep sleep.

I am very happy to announce that the Deva of Humanity has returned and is willing to work with humans again. It is no ordinary event; we have been waiting for this to happen for thousands of years, waiting and trying. I especially want to congratulate the volunteers who were responsible for making it happen with their dedication and perseverance. The Deva of Humanity has started trusting again. What a wonderful news for all of us. The event occurred in May of 2023 when the Deva of

Humanity finally showed their real self to dedicated and trustworthy volunteers. Earth is blessed to have these volunteers helping her during this time.

In this chapter, I want to emphasize the role of the Deva of Humanity. The future of humanity depends on it. For a golden future, the least we can do is seek guidance from the Deva of Humanity, maintain a good relationship with devas, and prove ourselves to be trustworthy to other kingdoms. This is the least humanity can do as part of the ascension process.

There are many things you can do to demonstrate you are a trustworthy member of the human family. Trustworthiness is synonymous with maintaining a good relationship with people from different countries, backgrounds, or cultures. Just like friends of different backgrounds than you, other kingdoms represent the Source, yet with different roles and ways to evolve. Devas have been close friends and companions of humans, showing lovingly their interest in initiating relationship with humans. Humans, on the other hand, have trust issues and try to be in control as a result of eons of deep conditioning. Deep conditioning has made humans miserable as they seek things outside, relying completely on technology, and forgetting their connection with the Source.

The first step would be for humans to consider themselves as a fragment of God. This definition might irritate a few because they have studied and learned differently from other people. Conditioning is what keeps you away from God. Conditioning is what tries to give you a false sense of belief in things that are human constructs. No one can change the essence of God, no matter what you believe. God will always remain in each one of us. It does not matter whether you can see it. Similarly, God is also seated in the beings of other kingdoms. They represent the Source as well—for example, the Source experiencing itself as deva kingdom.

The deva kingdom is one of the ancient kingdoms formed together with human souls. We were created at the same time and evolved together. Humanity reached Atlantis, and devas built the entire infrastructure for humanity to continue its evolutionary path. Then humanity thought of themselves to be above the deva kingdom. They tried to evolve further, leaving behind the devas, which made the Deva of Humanity very sad and betrayed. The Deva of Humanity abandoned the humans soon after and went into deep sleep.

Since the Deva of Humanity is back once again and has agreed to help humanity return to its path of evolution towards the Source, a lot of help in the form of spiritual growth solutions and guidance has become available. The Deva of Humanity can help humanity work together with devas and provide an opportunity to form a union with devas. The deva kingdom will hugely benefit from this since the Deva of Humanity will help them trust humans once again and build a community on trust, friendship, and a deep understanding of each other's role in their evolution. The Deva of Humanity speaks through certain volunteers and can be found at www.thedevaofhumanity.org. Please read the messages received from the Deva of Humanity and try to interpret them with your heart, not your head. Your heart will help you uncover the truth. Your head will lead you to darkness if not properly used in alignment with the divine. The Deva of Humanity will uncover the knowledge that had been lost to humanity for thousands of years – knowledge that was common during the time of Atlantis. The Deva of Humanity has our full support and trust that they will help humanity be in touch again with the Divine and Creation.

To think of the Deva of Humanity speaking directly to all of you is a tremendous achievement and a milestone in the ascension of humanity. We have already discussed with the Deva of Humanity what would be uncovered and when. It is a greatly discussed curriculum that the Deva of Humanity will cover in their messages. The Deva of Humanity was once part of the Council of Shambala, where their role was to discuss and bring any major concerns to Shambala that needed to be addressed by the SANAT

KUMARA and us. We worked very closely with her during the time of Atlantis. She was one of us. She had immense respect and care for humanity. She is an advanced soul who has been working with humanity and us for eons. Think of her as an old and ancient being like the SANAT KUMARA and other evolved souls who have seen multiple universes come and go. The Deva of Humanity has been working with us on various projects to establish trust between devas and humans, evolutionary milestones of humans and devas, and topics like the enhancement of the relationship between the various kingdoms and how to maintain it for the highest good of the Earth and its inhabitants.

The Deva Of Humanity's rebirth is a major milestone celebrated hugely by us at Shambala. The task from Shambala and us is to treat her with utmost respect and honour. Request her guidance when deemed necessary. She has taken a leap of faith to regain trust in humanity. Work together to show her that humanity lives up to her expectations and that humanity has hope of bringing back the golden time of Atlantis. One or two people doing this are not enough. Everyone has to reunite and come together for this task. With this chapter, my intention for you is to realize the importance of working together with devas and the Deva of Humanity. Together, we can earn their trust back, which is vital and critical in this ascension process.

MEANING OF LIFE, DEATH, AND BEYOND

The mystery of death might not be an alien concept to you. Many scriptures have their version of what happens during and after death. Many may be inclined to this topic since it interests them to learn more about the afterlife. For now, keep aside the knowledge you have gathered from other sources for a while since the knowledge I will provide you with now may or may not contradict what you have already learned. Only a few have come closer to the truth, and a handful of people actually understand this process completely with the reasoning of events during the process called *death* on Earth.

Death scares many people while others might be eager to leave Earth as soon as possible. The question remains: What happens to you after death? Death is a plain event like any other event where the soul decides to leave the body at will, and this might not be the will of the incarnated aspect but that of your soul, which you also refer to as the higher self.

As your soul decides to leave the body at will, the incarnated aspect of your soul is separated from the body by deva beings. Deva beings are the ones who design your costume or body. This is a very simple and fast process, much like you decide to change your clothes. It is neither a painful nor a complicated process and is as simple as removing old clothes. The reason death is feared by many is because of unknowingness – not knowing what happens next. Some have a concept of hell or heaven, while some think you reincarnate at the same moment somewhere else. Both of these assumptions are factually wrong. There is no heaven or hell, nor does your soul reincarnate immediately. There is a resting period given to your soul for healing.

You would not believe the number of souls getting healed

at the moment before coming to Earth; it's a huge number equivalent to the population of Earth. Among them, not everyone will get a chance to incarnate on Earth. Some will move to a different project for their evolution, but few will incarnate on Earth who will have important soul missions to accomplish along with their self-development mission.

Death is like removing a tight costume that you have worn for such a long time that you have adapted to it. It is a tight costume indeed, and that is how it feels for a soul when removing its costume. Then there is a moment of sigh and the soul is happy to be out of the tight costume it had worn for so long. The reason why I am telling you this is that there is nothing to fear about death. When a loved one or someone you know closely passes away, nothing happens to them, and their costume has been removed. This fear only brings you down and sometimes affects your soul mission. The passed-on soul may or may not be able to talk to you again, but it sure wishes that you remain focused on your soul mission. Many may get deeply affected by someone's death and decide to abandon their soul mission, but that will only do damage, not only to Earth but to your soul as well. Take it as a self-development lesson and work towards your soul mission; that is what we will advise you.

Speaking of death, I would like you to consider an example: It's about a person who volunteered to come to Earth, and like other volunteers, the person thought there was more to this world than just their regular job and life. The person read many books where people tried to explain the meaning of life. This person is each of you right now on Earth, trying to find your way and trying to find resources to help you understand life that resonates with you.

You think that life cannot be just phases of happiness and sadness to be experienced by you where you are just witnessing things happening to you. Let me tell you, it's not. Life is more than just patterns of happiness and sadness. It is here for a reason to teach you numerous lessons, and if you master these lessons beforehand, there will be no more lesson to learn and hence no sadness to experience, just you enjoying your life much like a visitor enjoys its ride. Sometimes, the ride takes a difficult turn, but that does not mean that the ride will break; it means enjoying the difficult turns of the ride like all parts of the ride gracefully since you are just a visitor of this ride. If you have mastered the lessons before, the difficult turns will not surprise you, nor will you feel sad facing these difficult turns. Hence, my message is that life is not a pattern of happiness and sadness. We feel sad if the self-development lessons are not mastered, but it will not affect you if you are already a master of dealing with these. Now, mind you, sometimes we feel we have mastered many lessons only to face a lot of difficulty when challenges come. You might not even be aware of which lessons you have not mastered. It isn't easy to assess oneself and define what lessons still remain. The lessons of attachments, dealing with uncertain situations, and maintaining calm even when something terrible happens are lessons mostly made aware of when they occur in life. Apart from that, many remain unaware of these lessons, and that is why difficult times are a blessing in disguise. They show us what lessons we have not dealt with yet, and they put a bright spotlight on areas that have been ignored. Difficult times are a gift to your soul. They help your soul understand what it needs to accomplish in order to move closer to the Source because only a soul who has mastered all lessons will be eligible to reconnect with the Source. It's a mandatory criterion put up by the Source in the game of life.

You must think what a terrible criterion it is to go through so many difficult times to reach the Source. I would say the criteria may sound harsh to you now, but when you see it from the bigger perspective, the soul goes through the experiences and is unaffected by them. It only collects the qualities exhibited by Source and nothing else. No event on Earth can change the core of the soul. The soul can only absorb the qualities, but at the core, the soul is a fragment of the Source, and nothing can ever happen for it to be not part of the Creator. The experiences may seem terrible at times, but please do understand what they offer. They offer a life to be lived by a formless being. Living a simple experience as a being with form is a gift for your soul that does not have a form. I hope my perspective has helped you understand what we achieve having difficult experiences. It is all part of the process, the process of life on Earth.

The concept of death is an important topic, and I want to spend some more time explaining the transition. We do not call it death on this side. We call it transition or cross-over because death means the end of life, whereas transition means leaving the old behind and entering another realm or home in this case. Many of you still do not know that our home is not dense physical; it is being in union with the Source. Considering the dense physical as your home is synonymous with considering taking exams as your home environment. You will not take tests forever. There will be breaks or changes in the test environment for you or changes in tests when you pass the current ones, but that does not make it your home. For many, fear of death comes from the idea of leaving everything and everyone in the dense physical behind, and that scares them because they are attached to their tests. Tests are meant to be forgotten when they are over. Attachment cannot change the outcome of a test, nor can it help you stay in the test environment longer. You have to come home today or tomorrow, it is inevitable. When you rest between incarnations, you let go of old attachment to it and think of new ways that can help you master pending tests that you were initially not able to accomplish. Once the rest period is completed, which is different for each soul, the soul has a new perspective on mastering lessons. Also, the soul sometimes makes brave decisions after long rest periods for their pending lessons. Guides then help them design their life on Earth – how they would look, which gender would be best to learn these lessons, the environment, and people who will help the soul or challenge it in order to master its new lessons.

These lessons are not generic for everyone and can mean anything like standing in power after abandonment; separating from a person to whom there is strong attachment, hence learning to let go; helping someone who has not been good to you; standing in your truth even when circumstances are against you; learning to love unconditionally or guiding less matured souls on their evolutionary journey. You see, these are examples of many lessons a soul can choose to accomplish. It is rare that two souls have the exact same lessons to undergo. There might be few similarities in one or two lessons, but during the incarnation journey, each soul has unique lessons to learn. Hence, it cannot be generalized for all.

Fear of death can be a lesson chosen by the soul to master. The transition or crossover is just like moving from one home to another. It is like coming home after a short journey on Earth; no matter how tough the journey might have been, you will always find the ticket to return to your home. Home is where you leave behind what was and relax. This is exactly what happens after coming home. You relax for some time, then go through what you accomplished and could not do. After going through your life, you take time to understand and relax before deciding to return. If you have mastered all lessons or most of them, then you are given a ticket to a higher class or grade where the environment and souls similar to you who have mastered previous lessons incarnate to master further lessons together. The new environment is different from the previous one in terms of the lessons it offers. For example, if you have mastered unconditional love in a previous environment, then in a new environment, everyone who incarnates has also mastered unconditional love and embodies those qualities of the Source. Similarly, if you have learned attachment and letting go, you will get a chance to incarnate where all souls have mastered attachment and then letting go.

The new environment may or may not be Earth. Earth is one of the billions of environments for souls to master their lessons. Some of the galaxies you know offer a new environment for souls who have learned their lessons on Earth. That does not make one environment better than the other. Each environment has its parameters and a lot to offer for incarnating souls. This knowledge is not alien to the soul. The soul has this knowledge and more, but I am imparting it because it has been forgotten on Earth. Incarnating aspects of souls used to have this knowledge, but with time after the fall of Atlantis, humanity had nothing to refer to for the history of Earth. Humanity could only find evidence of dinosaurs and other eras on Earth but never found its golden period of Atlantis, where the technology you have right now can be considered primary in comparison.

Similarly, the spiritual knowledge of souls was also well known, even to children. So you have to understand that this is nothing new, but I am trying to impart what you already knew once, when you were incarnated in Atlantis. During Atlantis, many researches were conducted, and in-depth discussions on these topics were conducted to understand soul evolution even further because it was primary knowledge.

Way back then, this knowledge was pretty common for everyone. So you understand how important it is to bring back this knowledge so that all incarnated aspects of souls are aware of their evolutionary journey and their role on Earth that they can fulfill, and hence accomplish the part they agreed to fulfill before coming to Earth.

Earth has been through many ups and downs, a lot of turbulence, as you may call it. A lot has changed since Atlantis. People have changed. Their ideologies and their perception of a good life have changed. Many aspire to become wealthy or famous. They are attached to dense physical constructs, similar to playing a video game and getting attached to coins offered in the game.

Wealth does not mean anything to your soul, nor does fame. Your soul aspires to evolve in terms of accomplishing tasks and lessons it came here to learn. Not fulfilling the missions you agreed to fulfill is worse than accumulating wealth and fame. Your tasks and lessons decide the outcome of this incarnation. If your soul could accomplish its tasks and master its lessons, it would not care about how much wealth was accumulated by its incarnated aspect in the dense physical. This is all part of social conditioning, where Earth has undergone various phases. The conditioning to please society and live by its rules, even if it does not resonate with your situation, has been persistent since the fall of Atlantis. You may not realize it, but there was a time on Earth during Atlantis when society only promoted what aligned with the truth of spirituality. Conditioning was almost negligible. Each soul knew the truth of God, the balance of nature, and other kingdoms on Earth. Everyone knew what was supposed to be done to live in harmony, unlike the current situation on Earth. My point is that we are not bringing the New Age; we are just returning to who we were. It is not something new to Earth. It is the realization that Earth already was in that age and wishes to transition back.

I hope this is helping you get a new perspective: We are going to the old ways of Atlantis, not to an age that would be alien to everyone where you all lived in harmony. You do not remember those lives due to the Earth's laws of forgetfulness. Before starting with the next lesson, I would like to tell you that the coming of the New Age has been in the works for centuries now, and this is the final stage where it will be completed for Earth. What does that mean for the entire population of Earth? The Earth as a whole will ascend with people who have high vibrations or have learned their lessons successfully and have been of service to Earth. These people will have no problem adjusting to new conditions. The main concern will be for people in the middle; neither have they completed all the lessons nor are they entirely towards the other end. A choice will need to be made by them. They will either have to consciously make efforts to raise their vibrations, learn more about spirituality, or completely adapt the other ways of service to self and leave this planet. Being in the middle will be difficult for them. They will not completely understand what is happening and will have a tough time digesting the information given by Ambassadors of Light. With our teachings, we want to make it easy for them to take a leap of faith and choose spirituality. Stranded in the middle will not be of any help. I hope my message reaches all of them and helps them calm themselves to decide before it gets too late.

THE MIND AND ITS GAMES

The mind, an integral part of the human body, can be destructive or helpful to one's soul in making life decisions. The soul does not make these decisions, but the mind of the human body. The soul does not have anything to do with the decisions you make in day-to-day life, like going for a walk, choosing food, or making big decisions like choosing a career path, or getting married. All these decisions are made by the mind. The soul can intervene in the form of guidance, nothing more and nothing less. The mind, being an integral part of the human body, is not part of your soul. Your soul observes the decisions made by your mind and every thought you have. The mind is not related to the soul at any level. That is why we talk of the 'mind and its games,' because it wants you to do what it thinks is right. A human mind cannot judge whether a situation is right for you, which is why soul guidance plays an important role in one's life. Without soul guidance, your life can turn out to be useless. Borrowing the beliefs of others may create more harm for you than help you.

Beliefs define an individual's life path. They are more important for your soul than you may think. Beliefs spread like wildfire, burning everything in the vicinity. You may think that borrowing beliefs from the world is wise since the world has everything figured out, or at least this is what they want you to think. An individual's belief system goes deep within oneself; it has layers and layers accumulated since childhood. The belief is that you have to earn good grades to make a place in this world, or else everyone will think you are inferior. The belief in being there for your family because you will be a bad father, mother, son, or daughter if you do not. These beliefs are not your soul's but are rather instilled in your mind. Your soul does not want to do things your mind may come up with.

Soul downloads are different. You receive an inspiration or idea to do something in alignment with your soul mission. These downloads generally occur out of random where there is no clear thought process of how you found that idea or inspiration. Soul downloads are a powerful way to receive soul guidance for your path even when you have not asked. Soul guidance plays a vital role for one's soul. It helps individuals reach their life path and help them evolve further to reach the Source. When activated, soul guidance can mean different things for an individual. It could mean letting go of everything you did not know was blocking your mission until your soul helped you clear it out. Soul guidance can sometimes be difficult to digest since an incarnated aspect of the soul might go down a road that the soul does not feel will help achieve its mission. Activation of soul guidance for some means swallowing the bitter truth of letting go of anything that seems to block your mission. Hence, it might become difficult for some when soul guidance is activated. The decisions that your soul tells you to take are greatly calculated decisions, even if no reasoning is provided. This requires trust, sometimes immense trust.

Soul guidance can be distinguished from the chatter of mind by one simple technique: When you receive your soul's guidance, there will be no emphasis on doing something. The emphasis is missing in soul guidance because your soul cannot emphasize taking certain actions. Rather, it provides you with clarity, a nudge, or a suggestion, a polite suggestion. You will know when speaking with your soul how polite it is. On the other hand, the mind may provide strong suggestions or emphasis on doing something which, if you do not try, will guilt-trip you into thinking that you are not following your soul's guidance. It is simple to distinguish between the two but not easy. The mind gives guidance with some strong ideas which you have to do and make logical sense. Mind guidance can try to masquerade as soul guidance. It might be harmless but can be destructive if you do not pay attention to your mind masquerading as your soul.

The soul is polite and gentle, whispers and suggests you do something. It can never tell you to do something directly. It suggests, often leaving it up to you to decide. Try this technique to identify if it is your soul's guidance or your mind trying to masquerade as your soul. Identifying this can be challenging, but it will be effortless once you start distinguishing and understanding the essence of your soul. Many great, enlightened beings have faced this challenge, so do not worry if you do not get it right initially. It is all divinely orchestrated. Receiving your soul's guidance is orchestrated by your soul.

It takes effort for an incarnated aspect of a soul to talk to its soul. Its guidance, even though destined and planned, can only be received if an incarnated aspect of the soul takes an effort. However, with small efforts, the soul tries to provide guidance in multiple ways, which your mind may or may not interpret depending upon which way the soul has chosen. These ways are not straightforward communication between you and your soul, but it can be as simple as a sign from your guides nudging you to initiate something. This is soul guidance. It might seem less reliable since the incarnate aspect may or may not interpret it as a sign to do something and may reject it as something that is a mere coincidence. The interpretation of signs is usually for those who are spiritually more open and perceptive. These people usually capture these signs easily. Whether they act on them or not is a different thing. It is a gift to understand signs from your guides through nudges.

Made in the USA
Middletown, DE
14 October 2023